Birds and Their Nests

by Linda Cernak

Harcourt
SCHOOL PUBLISHERS

Cover, ©James Warwick/The Image Bank/Getty Images; p.3 (tr), ©Scott T. Smith/CORBIS, (tl) (bl) ©Corel, (br) ©PhotoDisc; p.4, ©Fritz Polking; Frank Lane Picture Agency/CORBIS; p.5, ©Dennis Flaherty/Photographer's Choice/Getty Images; p.6, ©Jan Tove Johansson/Taxi/Getty Images; p.7, ©WIM KLOMP/FOTO NATURA/Minden Pictures; p.8, p.11, p.14, ©Corel; p.9, ©Kennan Ward/ CORBIS; p.10, ©PhotoDisc; p.12, ©Nigel J. Dennis/Photo Researchers, Inc.; p.13, ©Frans Lemmens/ zefa/Corbis.

Printed in China

ISBN 10: 0-15-351512-0
ISBN 13: 978-0-15-351512-5

Ordering Options
ISBN 10: 0-15-351213-X (Grade 3 Advanced Collection)
ISBN 13: 978-0-15-351213-1 (Grade 3 Advanced Collection)
ISBN 10: 0-15-358102-6 (package of 5)
ISBN 13: 978-0-15-358102-1 (package of 5)

4 5 6 7 8 9 10 985 12 11 10 09 08

Birds come in a large variety of sizes and shapes, and so do their nests. You might think that all bird nests are the same, but they're not. Bird nests are as different as the birds that build them. Nests can be very tiny, or nests can be extremely large. Nests are built in many different places, too. You might find a nest in a small bush, a tall tree, or even on the top of a mountain.

Birds lay different numbers of eggs in a nest, too. Some nests will hold ten to fifteen eggs at one time!

Birds know exactly what materials to look for to create their nests. Birds may use grasses, twigs, sticks, and feathers. Some birds use moss or mud to line their nests and keep them warm.

Birds will use just about anything to build a nest. Nests have been found with strands of paper and string woven into them. Pieces of wool, foil, and balls of animal hair are found in many nests. A bird may make hundreds of trips to get all the supplies it requires for its nest.

Once the bird has collected everything it needs to make its nest, then it's time to finish it up. Many bird nests are built in the shape of a cup. To finish its cup nest, the bird sits in the pile of supplies that it has gathered. The bird then turns around in circles and reels in the materials. As the bird turns, it pushes the pieces of the nest into place. Soon the inside of the nest is shaped exactly like a cup!

A stork's nest

A favorite place for a bird to create a cup nest is where the branches of a tree meet. You might even see a cup nest hanging from the branch of a tree. The bird fixes the nest to the tree by weaving the top of the nest around the branches.

A bird will build a nest just about anywhere, even on top of chimneys! Storks have been known to build nests on the tops of houses. Small birds, such as swallows and martins, build mud nests that cling to the ledges of buildings or walls.

Many birds build nests in very tall trees or in the thick of bushes. These well-hidden nests protect the young birds from animals that might prey upon them. Other birds hide their nests in holes in the trunks of trees.

You might have heard the rat-tap-tap of a woodpecker. The woodpecker carves a hole in the trunk of a tree with its sharp bill, and then when the hole is big enough, the woodpecker will build a nest there.

woodpecker

penguin

Some birds that live near the shore will dig a shallow hole in the ground and then lay their eggs in it. This hole is called a scrape. Some penguins build their nests on the ground, too. They make a pile of stones with a hole in the center, and there the female lays the eggs. Then the male penguin keeps the eggs warm.

Some nests are built high up on cliffs so that animals can't reach the nests and harm the eggs. Swallows and eagles build their nests on cliffs.

Another kind of nest that birds build is called a platform nest. It is a flat, simple nest. A platform nest might be built on the ground, or you might even observe a platform nest floating on the top of water in a swamp. Large birds such as herons and ospreys usually build platform nests. The birds create a small hole in the nest in order to lay their eggs.

heron

An eagle in its nest

The hummingbird's nest is tiny, no bigger than a tablespoon! That's because the hummingbird egg is extremely small—approximately the size of a jellybean!

Eagles build enormous nests in the branches of giant trees. An eagle's nest is called an aerie, and it consists of large branches, sticks, and sometimes cornstalks. Eagles line the nests with weeds, moss, and pieces of dirt with grass stuck in it. The nests are large, almost 5 feet (1.52 m) across and 2 feet (.61 m) high! Eagles will return each year and use the same nest to lay their eggs.

Some birds build their nests on special plants. A reed warbler builds its nest on the long stalks of a reed plant. Reeds are tall plants that grow in swamps. The nest hangs onto the reeds like a basket, and the birds weave reed flowers, grass, and feathers to make a cup-shaped nest.

Some birds actually create their nests from mud! A swallow often builds mud nests inside barns or garages. The birds enter the barns through cracks or open windows, and the nests are built attached to walls.

A mud nest

Weaverbirds live in Asia and in Africa. They are known for building nests in various shapes. Most weaverbirds build their nests by tying strips of grass into knots. The birds work with their bills and their claws. The birds build the outside of the nest first, and then they finish the inside. The finished nest looks like a large ball hanging from between branches of a tree.

One kind of weaverbird builds a nest that looks like a long spiral tunnel. The opening to the nest is at the bottom to keep snakes from trying to reach the eggs at the top.

Village weaverbirds are very social birds. Hundreds of village weaverbirds might build nests in the same tree! Each pair of male and female birds has its own nest.

Another kind of weaverbird lives in large groups. They build nests that are like apartment houses. A weaverbird nest looks like a large straw cone, and hundreds of birds may live in it. Each pair of birds has its own hollow space in the nest. Some nests can be as big as 10 feet (3.05 m) high and 15 feet (4.57 m) across!

With many kinds of birds, males and females both participate in creating the nests. They also share in caring for their young. Many young birds are born without feathers and with their eyes shut. Before long the baby birds open their eyes. The baby birds grow bigger every day, feathers begin to appear, and the baby birds learn to fly. Before long the young birds leave the nests. Eventually, they will build nests of their own.

Think Critically

1. Why do some birds build their nests on cliffs?

2. Why do you think a penguin makes a nest with a pile of rocks instead of leaves and branches?

3. Why do different birds build different kinds of nests?

4. With what kinds of materials do birds make their nests?

5. Which bird in the book did you find most interesting? Explain.

Science

Make a Nest Imagine that you are a bird who needs to build a nest. Decide what materials you would use and why. Then draw a detailed diagram of your nest.

 School-Home Connection Talk with a family member about the birds that live in your neighborhood. Did you see any birds on your way home from school? Watch for some next time.